Given to:

_____

From:

_____

Date:

_____

Our Baby Book

Our Baby Book

Illustrated by

Caron Turk

BAKER
A DIVISION OF
Baker Book House Co

NEW
Kids
MEDiA ®

Place a copy of your baby announcement here

Children are a *gift* from the Lord; they are a *reward* from him.

Psalm 127:3

♥ Our Precious Baby ♥

- -

was born on

- -

to

- -

and

- -

♥ Place photo here ♥

Will you have Mama's smiling eyes
or Grandma's turned up nose,
Daddy's curly hair or Grandpa's skinny toes?
We can't wait to get to know you and see who you become.
One thing is absolutely certain...
you've been ♥loved♥ from DAY ONE!

In the Beginning...

Love

Baby Baby

(Place photos of Mom and Dad when they were babies.)

First there was one, then there were two.

LOVE

BABY

MOM

Dad

Miracle of miracles, now there is YOU.

How Mom and Dad met.....

♥ Some of their friends are...

♥ Where they work...

All About

Grandma & Grandpa

on Mom's Side

All About

Grandma & Grandpa

on Dad's Side

When We First Found Out You Were On Your Way....

Every good and perfect gift is from above. James 1:17

(Place first sonogram photo here.)

(Place photo of Mom just before baby was born.)

You are bone of my bone and flesh of my flesh.
Genesis 2:23

Photos

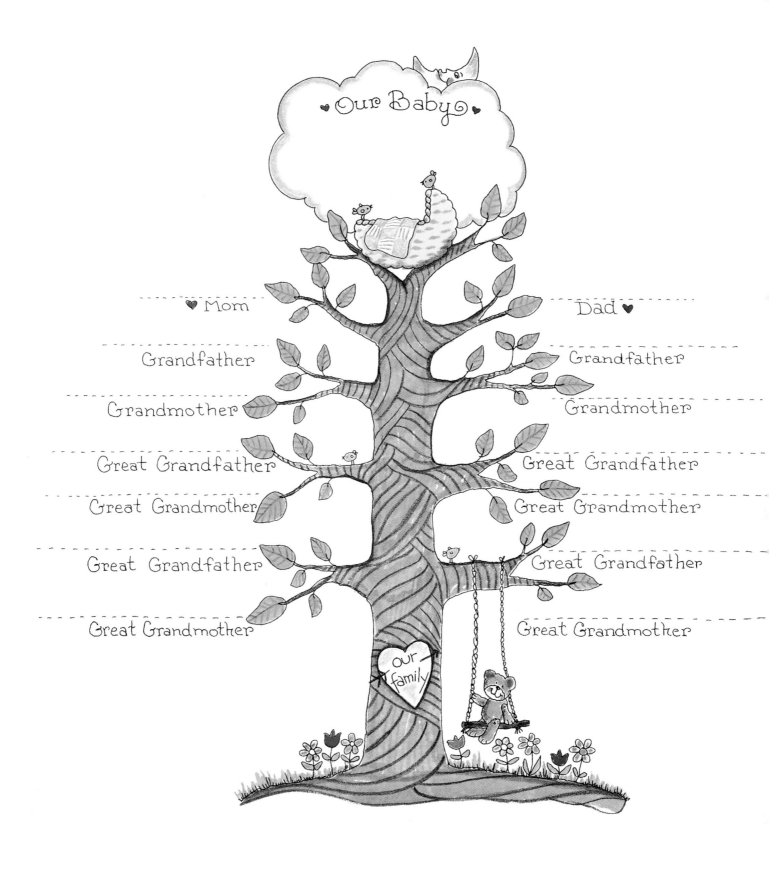

...more special family members...

Parties to Welcome You!

Baby · Baby · Baby

❤ Who gave the shower

🐤 The theme was

❤ Who came

🎁 Gifts

Parties

More Parties

_____

_____

_____

_____

_____

_____

_____

_____

_____

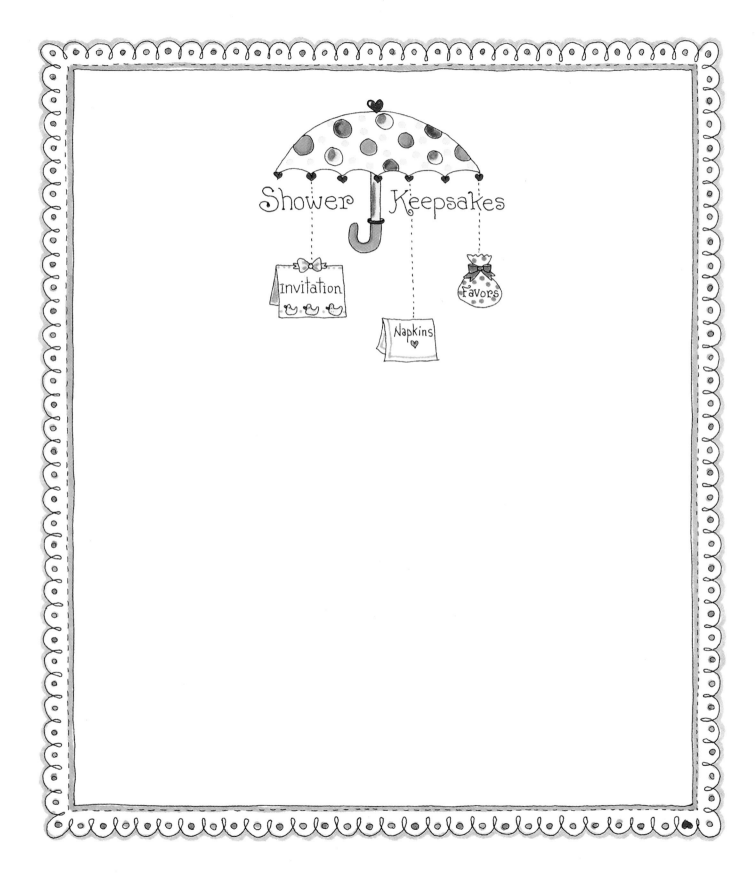

Shower Keepsakes

Invitation

Napkins

Favors

Mom's Cravings

yum!

Mom's favorite pregnant clothes...

The most comfortable way for Mom to sleep...

z z z

Welcome home, baby

What Your "Birth" ⭐ Day Was Like...

❤ Things Mom did that day...

❤ Where you were born...

❤ Doctor or Midwife's name...

❤ What the weather was like...

❤ What time you arrived...

❤ You weighed...

❤ You were this long...

❤ Your actual due date was...

❤ Did you have hair? ...yes ...no
What color?

❤ Your eyes were...

Your First Picture

(Place photo here)

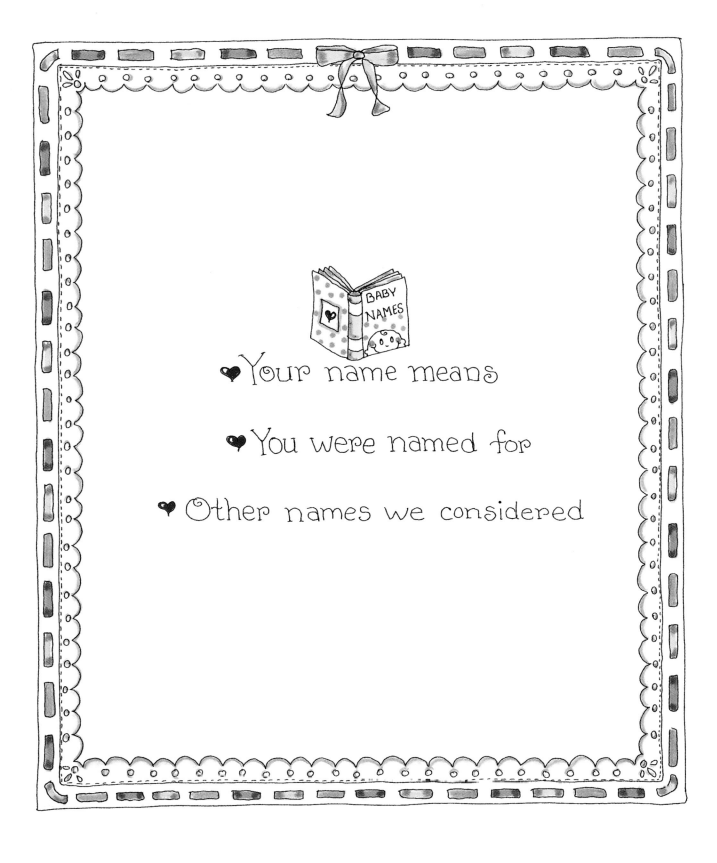

♥ Your name means

♥ You were named for

♥ Other names we considered

Footprints

date

Handprints

date

There Was News Besides You?

You've ARRIVED! 25¢
• NEWS •

⭐ .... was the president when you were ♥ born.

⭐ Some popular television shows were...

⭐ Popular movies were...

⭐ Top songs and performers were...

⭐ Fabulous fashions and fads were...

⭐ Star professional athletes were...

Extra Extra

The Big News of the Day!

(Place the headline from the local newspaper here)

Other Interesting Stuff

What did things cost?

- Gallon of milk...
- Loaf of bread...
- Candy bar...
- Postage stamp...
- Gallon of gas...

(Place copy of birth certificate here)

News Too Good to Keep to Ourselves!

♥ The first people we called were...

♥ Some things they said...

Mom's View of Your Birth Day

Dad's View of Your Birth Day

Baby

Your ♥ Nursery

(Place photo of room here)

welcome

Your first visitors were...

Baby

The Outfit You Wore Home Was...

♥ What was the weather like?

♥ What kind of car did Mom and Dad drive?

How did Mom and Dad feel about bringing you home? ♥

Special gifts ♥
& cards you received...

say "cheese"

♥ Pictures of your first few days at home ♥

Mom with you...♥

Dad with you...♥

Grandma & Grandpa
     with you...♥

Photos

Magnificent "Firsts"

🚗 Trip outside of home

🐤 Bath

⛪ Church

📝 Babysitter

☕ Restaurant visit

🍼 Shopping trip

♥••• More Magnificent Firsts ♥••♥

♥ Smile

♥ Rolled over

♥ Laughed

♥ Slept through the night

♥ Solid food

♥ Crawled

Even More!

- ❤ Sat up

- ❤ Pulled up

- ❤ Stood up

- ❤ First steps

- ❤ First tooth

- ❤ First word

- ❤ Said "Mama" and/or "Daddy"

- ❤ First boo-boo

OUCH!

First ♥ Haircut

♥

(Put a piece of hair in an
envelope and tape here)

Baby's Favorite Things

Toys

Books

Blankie

Pacifier

Snack & food

Your Favorite Things to Do with Mom

♥ Naptime routine

♥ Books to read

♥ Songs Mom sings to you

♥ How Mom makes you laugh

Favorite Things to Do with Dad

- ❤ Bedtime routine

- ❤ Books to read

- ❤ Games to play

Baby's Growth Chart

Age	Weight		Height	
	Lbs.	Oz.	Ft.	In.
Birth				
One Month				
Two Months				
Three Months				
Four Months				
Five Months				
Six Months				
Seven Months				
Eight Months				
Nine Months				
Ten Months				
Eleven Months				
Twelve Months				
Eighteen Months				
Twenty-four Months				

"Sooo Big"

Special Notes
All about Baby

Your First Doctor Visit

Questions Mom & Dad asked...

Drs.
Notes...
Wt.
Length

What the doctor said about you...

Photos

Special Days We Celebrate
♥ All Year Long ♥

Winter

Spring

Summer

FaLL

Baby's First Christmas

- ❤ How we celebrated

- ❤ What you wore

- ❤ Gifts

- ❤ What you thought of the decorations

Happy Easter Baby

♥ How we celebrated

♥ What you wore

(photo of baby)

Jesus said, "Let the little children come to me."
Mark 10:14 (NIV)

Jesus Is Alive

Happy First Birthday

♥ Theme...

♥ Who came...

Cake... Did you eat messy or neat?

♥ Who came to your party?

Photos of Your Party

Special FRIENDS

♥ What you like to play with friends...

♥ Favorite "treat"...

Trace baby's hands on this page

Notes from Special ♥ People...

♥ Message from Mom

♥ Message from Dad

♥ Message from Grandma

♥ Message from Grandpa

Dear Baby,
You are so special, and dear, a blessing...

more special messages for baby

Happy  Birthday

2nd

Theme...

Cake...

Who helped you celebrate...

Gifts...

Favorite Friends this Year...

Sooooo Big!

trace child's hands here...

Happy 3rd Birthday

🎉 Theme...

🎂 Cake...

🎈 Who helped you celebrate...

🎁 Gifts...

Happy Birthday to You!

say cheese!

Party ♥ Photos

Favorite Friends this Year...

my favorite friends

Sooooo Big!

trace child's hands here...

Happy **Birthday**

4th

Theme...

Cake...

Who helped you celebrate...

Gifts...

Happy Birthday to You!

Say cheese!

Party ♥ Photos

Favorite Friends this Year...

Sooooo Big !

trace child's hands here...

Happy  Birthday

5th

Theme...

Cake...

Who helped you celebrate...

Gifts...

Favorite Friends this Year...

Sooooo Big!

trace child's hands here...